Revive Your Clinic Revenue

Bold Leaders: Stop the Bleeding, Crush Denials, and Build Financially Unbreakable Practices

By Flora Sanders, CMRM

Heal Your Cash Flow, Stop Claim Denials, and Reclaim Your Clinic's Financial Health

First Edition: 2025
Printed in the United States of America

ISBN: 978-1-968110-01-7
Library of Congress Control Number:

Published by LSanders Publishing

This book is a work of nonfiction. All stories and case studies are based on real experiences (with identifying details changed) or inspired by common professional scenarios. Any resemblance to real people, living or dead, is purely coincidental unless explicitly acknowledged.

For permissions, services, speaking engagements, or bulk orders, please contact:
Revive Revenue Services
Flora.Sanders@ReviveRevenueServices.com
ReviveRevenueServices.com

Dedication

"You cannot heal what you refuse to confront.
You cannot build what you will not lead."

—

For the leaders who refuse to watch their clinics
bleed out.

For the fighters who choose precision over
excuses.

For the builders who will not let their mission die
from hidden wounds.

This is your BOLD battle plan.

This is your time.

Lead boldly. Lead now.

Note to Bold Leaders

Your clinic's revenue cycle is not just unhealthy; it is bleeding internally, silently, and invisibly, and if left untreated, the collapse will be sudden and irreversible.

This is a scenario of you dealing with more than a mild inconvenience; you are dealing with trauma.

Consider the following … what if:

… Every denied claim is a laceration?

… Every missed verification is a severed artery?

… Every one of your aging receivables is a hidden infection spreading deeper into your financial system?

Like your patients, you can no longer pretend the bleeding will stop by itself. You can no longer hope that your clinic will "pull through" without some type of intervention.

You must act.

5

The first step is emergency triage: Stop the bleeding. Stabilize the patient. Diagnose the unseen damage, but triage is not enough. Emergency treatment saves lives, but it does not rebuild futures.

Once you stabilize your clinic's financial health, you must begin a second, equally critical journey: You must drive your clinic toward full operational recovery and future-proof strength. You need a roadmap.

Without it, you will drift. Without it, you will crash. Without it, you will repeat the cycle of emergency after emergency until your mission of exceptional patient care fractures beyond repair.

Don't think about this book as just a first aid manual or a light touch. It is for bold leaders. It is your complete battle plan and navigation chart.

It shows you exactly how to stabilize, rebuild, and accelerate, step by step, checkpoint by checkpoint, until your clinic becomes financially unbreakable.

It is time to stop the bleeding and stabilize the patient. It is time to take the wheel, plot your course, and drive relentlessly toward financial dominance.

The trauma ends when you confront it. The journey begins when you lead it.

Welcome to your REVIVAL.

Table of Contents

A Promise to the Bold Leader

Medicine is serious business. The business of medicine is just as serious.

Your clinic exists to heal people, but its ability to do so depends on its financial strength.

Think of this as being not just about balance sheets or billing cycles. The success of your clinic is not only a win for you and your staff, but it is a lifeline for every patient who counts on your expertise.

That is why this book is more than a casual read. It is a wake-up call. If your clinic is in financial intensive care, we will begin the healing. If it is already healthy, we will take it to a level of fitness and resilience most practices never reach.

The truths you are about to read will be blunt. They will be uncomfortable, but they will be real, and if you are willing to face them, your clinic will never be the same again.

You are about to confront brutal financial truths.

You are about to face the reality that your clinic is bleeding more revenue than you realize.

You are about to see that operational inefficiency is more than a minor nuisance because it is a life-threatening condition, but if you stay in this fight, if you act on what you learn, you will come out the other side stronger than you ever thought possible.

Here is my promise to you:

If you engage fully with openness and honesty, and continued hunger for improvements, if you refuse to settle for excuses, if you lead with urgency and precision, and if you execute, then you will:

Stop the silent bleeding. Rebuild your clinic's financial core. Lead an organization that is financially unbreakable, operationally unstoppable, and future-proofed against any challenge.

You will not just survive the chaos in healthcare.

You will dominate it.

This book is not theory, it is action.

This is not optional; it is crucial.

This is your leadership moment.

The future belongs to the **bold,** and it starts now.

– Flora Sanders, CMRM

Foreword

The future of healthcare will not be decided by clinical excellence alone. It will be decided by the leaders who master the financial engines of their organizations with as much intensity, strategy, and courage as they bring to patient care.

Flora Sanders, CMRM, has written the manual that every clinic leader needs at this critical crossroads. *Revive Your Clinic Revenue* is not another polite guide full of suggestions. It is a hard-hitting manifesto that forces readers to confront the brutal realities of their operational weaknesses and equips them to build something unbreakable in their place.

I have seen firsthand the difference between clinics that treat Revenue Cycle Management (RCM) as a strategic imperative and those that treat it as an afterthought. The former thrive. The latter struggle endlessly, leaking cash, burning out staff, and forfeiting their futures inch by inch.

This book calls leaders to a higher standard. It does not pander. It does not apologize for demanding excellence. It tells the bold truth: you either master your revenue cycle, or it masters you.

Mrs. Sanders challenges clinic leaders to act with urgency, precision, and relentless discipline. She exposes the silent killers lurking in everyday operations. She lays out a clear, executable framework for diagnosis, remedy, and transformation, and she does it all with a voice that is refreshingly direct, fiercely practical, and unmistakably committed to results.

Reading this book will force you to ask the hard questions:

- Are you tolerating "average" because excellence feels too hard?

- Are you blind to the real financial bleeding happening every day?

- Are you willing to lead boldly enough to fix it?

If you are not ready to lead differently, stop reading now, but if you are ready to break free from mediocrity, to reclaim control over your clinic's future, and to build a revenue cycle strong enough to fuel your highest mission, then turn the page.

This is the new standard. Your clinic's survival and success depend on what you do next.

[Supporter's Name]
[Supporter's Title or Credentials]
[Supporter's Organization]

Preface

Too many clinics today are in financial trouble, not because they lack patients, talent, or opportunity, but because they lack the operational capability or courage to confront the brutal realities of their business.

The problem is not "out there" in the marketplace or with changing regulations. The problem is inside: outdated revenue cycle practices, weak leadership accountability, and a dangerous tolerance for mediocrity.

Every day denial rates go unchecked, aging receivables balloon, and patient balances grow uncollected, another piece of a clinic's future quietly dies. Yet, too many leaders allow it to happen because confronting hard truths is uncomfortable. Because change demands action. Because admitting there is a problem means accepting responsibility.

This book was not written for those who feel comfortable. It was written for the courageous.

You will not find fluff here. You will not find wishful thinking. You will find a hard-edged blueprint for leaders willing to do what others will not, and that is, face their numbers, fix what is broken, and forge an unstoppable future.

We are at a crossroads. Clinics that master the financial engine behind healthcare will thrive. Those who hesitate will disappear. The question is not if change is coming. It is whether you will lead it or be crushed by it.

Too many books treat revenue cycle improvement as an administrative afterthought. A "necessary evil." A boring technical domain.

They are wrong. Mastery of the revenue cycle is mastery of the clinic itself. It is operational discipline. It is leadership accountability. It is strategic dominance.

A clinic without financial strength is a clinic without options. Without options, patient care suffers. Staff morale craters. Growth opportunities vanish. Vision dies.

You have a choice. This book will help you make the right one. Bold leadership is no longer optional. It is survival.

The clinics that will dominate the next decade will not be those with the flashiest marketing or the fanciest buildings. They will be the ones with awesome patient care, and financial foundations so strong, so disciplined, so precise, that no competitor can match their resilience, agility, or strategic firepower.

Welcome to the movement. Welcome to the REVIVE System.

The REVIVE Framework:

- **Rapid Front-End Precision:** Patient registration, insurance verification, eligibility confirmation are all done right, the first time, every time. Revenue protection begins at the front desk.

- **Eliminate Denial Sources:** Root-cause analysis of every denied claim. Systematic eradication of recurring issues. Denials are not random. They are engineered by broken processes and tolerated by weak leadership.

- **Verify Claims Before Submission:** No claim leaves your system unchecked. No error slips through unnoticed. Clean claims are the currency of a financially healthy practice.

- **Invest in Smart Automation:** Technology is not optional. It is your competitive advantage. Automate what can be automated. Free up human talent for high-value tasks.

- **Visualize Metrics Relentlessly:** If you cannot measure it, you cannot manage it. Real-time visibility into denial rates, accounts receivable (A/R) aging, collections, and productivity is non-negotiable.

- **Engage Patients Financially Early:** Financial transparency before, during, and after care. Patient loyalty begins with financial clarity and convenience.

This is more than just a framework. It is a manifesto for operational and financial excellence.

The clinics that adopt the REVIVE Framework will dominate their local markets. They will have the cash flow to invest in growth, the strategic flexibility to outmaneuver competitors, and the operational discipline to weather any storm.

The clinics that do not will struggle. They will drown in denials, delayed payments, and administrative chaos. They will lose their best staff. They will watch patients drift away. They will become statistics.

There are no neutral outcomes.

Financial strength is not a luxury. It is the fuel for everything you hope to achieve. It funds better patient care. It funds staff development. It funds facility improvements, new technologies, and expanded services.

Without financial strength, your clinic becomes vulnerable to every external shock within your organization, like payer changes, regulatory shifts, economic downturns, and competitive encroachment. With it, your clinic becomes unbreakable.

The leadership required to achieve this is not soft. It is not passive. It is bold, disciplined, and relentless.

This book will challenge you. It will ask you to confront uncomfortable truths. It will force you to measure what you would rather ignore. It will expose the gaps between the clinic you have and the clinic you could build.

It will give you the tools to close that gap.

The path is clear:

Diagnose your weaknesses.

Implement the REVIVE Framework.

Demand excellence at every level. Execute relentlessly.

The leaders who act will not only survive. They will lead.

This is your moment.

Master the system. Build the team. Execute the strategy.

Lead without apology.

Build something extraordinary.

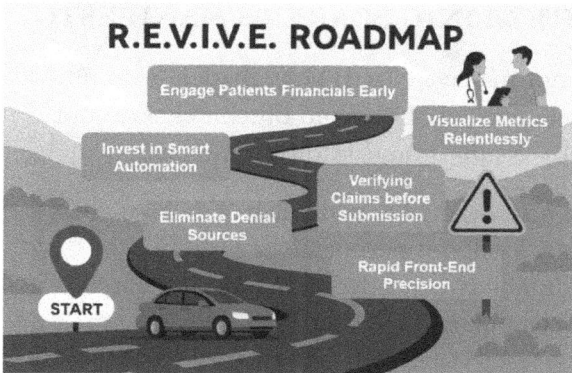

R.E.V.I.V.E. ROADMAP

The **REVIVE System** for Revenue Mastery

R: Rapid Front-End Precision

E: Eliminate Denial Sources

V: Verify Claims Before Submission

I: Invest in Smart Automation

V: Visualize Metrics Relentlessly

E: Engage Patients Financially Early

Your Revenue Cycle Is a Journey. Without a Map, You Will Crash. With This Book, You Will Drive Straight to Financial Strength and Leadership Victory.

THE CLINIC LEADER'S MANIFESTO

I do not manage chaos; I eliminate it. I do not tolerate excuses; I demand outcomes. I do not lead by assumption; I lead by metrics.

I will not allow poor systems to sabotage great people. I will not permit silence where accountability is needed. I will not let fear dictate financial failure.

I inspect what I expect. I measure what matters. I track what's broken, and I fix it.

I will ask the uncomfortable questions. I will name the inconvenient truths. I will lead meetings that result in action; not just discussion.

If something is failing, I will own it. If someone is struggling, I will coach them. If a process is broken, I will fix it.

I will walk the claim. I will follow the numbers. I will demand clarity, enforce excellence, and lead from the front.

The revenue cycle is not someone else's job; it's mine. Because my clinic's future is not someone else's responsibility; it's mine. Leadership is not a title; it's a decision I make every day.

I lead the numbers. I lead the people. I lead the systems. This is my clinic. This is my calling. This is my REVIVAL.

Intro
The Hidden
Revenue Crisis in
Clinics

Unless you have your finger firmly on the pulse of your business operations, you are already losing more money than you think.

The silent financial crisis in clinics is not coming someday, it is here now. Every day that denial rates go unchecked, every day that unpaid claims age and rot on the ledger, every day patient balances are ignored, the foundation beneath your clinic quietly erodes. It does not happen in a dramatic collapse. It happens slowly, silently, invisibly, until one day the entire structure gives way.

Most clinic leaders do not even realize they are standing on quicksand. They see the symptoms like cash flow shortfalls, frustrated billing staff, and mounting patient complaints, but these are treated as isolated problems. They patch symptoms instead of curing the disease. They hope next quarter will somehow be different.

Hope is not a strategy. Hope is how clinics die.

The truth is brutal, but the majority of revenue loss in healthcare is preventable. It is engineered not by external forces but by internal failures like poor systems, weak processes, lack of accountability, outdated technology, and leadership inertia.

Ask most clinic executives about their revenue cycle, and you will hear variations of the same rationalizations:

"Our denial rate is about average."

"Our A/R days could be better, but we are busy."

"Collections are a little slow, but patients are struggling."

The truth is that "average" in healthcare Revenue Cycle Management (RCM) is a disaster. Average denial rates mean millions left uncollected. Average A/R days mean cash flow strangulation. Average patient collection rates mean lost loyalty and increased bad debt.

Denials are not random. Aging A/R is not inevitable. Slow collections are not "just how it is." These are the visible signs of operational decay and leadership drift.

If you are not attacking your revenue cycle with the same intensity you bring to patient care, you are already losing the battle for your clinic's future.

You must break the cycle. You must reject "average". You must lead your clinic to a standard of operational and financial excellence that most organizations will never even attempt.

This book exists to wake you up before it is too late. It is your guide to doing exactly that.

We are not here to "optimize." We are here to radically transform.

Before We Begin: Face Your Numbers. Own Your Future.

Leadership is not about working harder. It is about producing better results. Results are always visible in your numbers.

Before you read another chapter, stop.

Pull your last ninety days or more of operational and financial data:

- What is your current revenue growth rate?

- What percentage of claims are denied on first submission?

- How many days does it take to collect payment after service?

- What percentage of patient balances are unpaid past thirty days?

- How many staff hours are wasted fixing avoidable billing errors?

- How many patient complaints trace back to billing confusion?

Document the truth. No spin. No excuses. No hiding.

Then answer one brutal question:

If these numbers do not radically improve in the next six months, what happens to your clinic, your staff, your patients?

Will you have the cash flow to grow? Will you have the reserves to withstand an external shock? Will your best staff stay if operations continue to frustrate them? Will patients stay loyal if billing friction grows?

You cannot lead from assumptions. You must lead from facts. You cannot fix what you do not measure. You cannot claim victory over problems you cannot name.

This is your leadership line in the sand.

Face your numbers. Own your future or lose your vision of exceptional patient care.

What This Book Will Teach You

Over the coming chapters, you will learn:

- How to diagnose the hidden weaknesses sabotaging your revenue cycle.

- How to leverage the REVIVE Framework and rebuild your financial operations from the ground up.

- How to design front-end processes that eliminate denials before they start.

- How to build a denial management system that recovers lost revenue and stops future leaks.

- How to modernize your patient financial engagement to maximize collections and loyalty.

- How to harness automation, AI, and analytics to drive precision and scale.

- How to choose the right RCM partners without getting trapped in costly mistakes.

- How to future-proof your clinic's financial engine against an increasingly volatile healthcare landscape.

This is not a theoretical exploration. This is a practical battle plan for leaders ready to execute.

Each chapter will challenge you. Each chapter will give you tools. Each chapter will move you closer to mastery or expose gaps you can no longer ignore.

The clinics that act on these principles will thrive. The clinics that hesitate will shrink, struggle, and disappear.

Commit now to be one of the former.

A Final Word Before We Begin

I just want to stress that this is not about minor tweaks nor about "doing a little better."

This is about taking bold control of your clinic's future. It is about building a financial engine strong enough to fund your vision and dreams, your mission, and your legacy.

Weak leadership will be crushed by the forces reshaping healthcare.

Bold leadership will rise.

If you are ready to be the leader your clinic, your staff, and your patients need and deserve, then turn the page.

Your financial revolution begins now.

Chapter 1
Exposing Revenue
Black Holes

Just like the bleeding of a trauma patient, every clinic bleeds revenue. The question is whether you know where and whether you have the courage to stop it.

Most clinic leaders believe their biggest financial threats come from external forces: shrinking insurance reimbursements, tightening regulations, and patients struggling to pay. They are wrong.

The biggest threats come from within.

The silent killers inside your clinic, those small daily operational failures, outdated billing processes, denial mismanagement, front-end sloppiness, are doing more damage to your cash flow, your reputation, and your future than any insurance company or government policy ever could.

Here is the brutal truth:

You are either actively eliminating your revenue black holes every month, or they are quietly eating you alive.

The slow bleed rarely feels urgent at first. Just like a patient who experiences body discomforts, mild at first, and then they accelerate.

A few denials here. A slight dip in collections there. A few months of high A/R aging. Always "fixable later." Always "not that bad."

Until one day, you realize you are sprinting harder just to stay afloat. Your cash reserves are vanishing. Your best staff are burning out. Your patient satisfaction is slipping. Your competitors are pulling ahead, and you are standing still, bleeding out.

No clinic collapses in what seems like overnight. The collapse is caused by a thousand cuts tolerated for too long.

This chapter will expose the most common and dangerous revenue black holes hiding inside clinics today. It will show you where the bleeding starts and how, if left unchecked, it leads to collapse.

It will not be comfortable, but it will be necessary.

Where Revenue Bleeds Start: The Unseen Front Lines

Most revenue leaks do not start in the billing department. They start at the front desk.

Every missed insurance verification, every incomplete patient intake, every failure to collect upfront copays sets off a cascade of chaos that eventually shows up as lost revenue.

Front-end failures multiply downstream, creating denials, payment delays, and patient confusion that could have been prevented.

If your front desk team does not operate with military-grade precision, you are bleeding money before the patient even sees the doctor.

Your front-end processes should be as disciplined and methodical as a trauma bay team preparing for surgery. No room for assumptions.

No room for "we forgot." No room for "we were too busy."

You cannot fix what you do not inspect and measure. If you have not audited your front-end processes in the last 90 days, you are flying blind and bleeding cash at high altitude.

Denials: The Expensive Outcome of Operational Neglect

Denials are not random acts of payer hostility. They are the predictable consequences of operational failure.

Wrong codes. Missing authorizations. Eligibility errors. Documentation gaps. All preventable. All costing you real money.

The industry average denial rate in healthcare hovers around 7 to 10 percent. Clinics operating at financial excellence push that below 3 percent. Every single percentage point matters.

Do the math. If your clinic processes $5 million a year in claims, and you can shave your denial rate from 10 percent to 3 percent, you reclaim $350,000 in revenue annually.

If you do not have a system for:

- Analyzing your denials by root cause,

- Prioritizing preventable categories,

- Systematically eliminating them,

… then you are voluntarily forfeiting hundreds of thousands of dollars every single year.

Denials are not "normal." They are self-inflicted wounds. Treat them as such.

Aging A/R: The Silent Killer of Cash Flow

If your accounts receivables (A/R) over 90 days exceeds 15 percent of your total A/R, your clinic is at financial risk.

Aging A/R chokes cash flow, creates your administrative chaos, and forces you into a reactive scramble to keep operations running. Worse, the longer a balance sits unpaid, the lower your chance of ever collecting it.

You must know, at all times:

- What percentage of your A/R is over 30, 60, and 90 days?

- What is the average time to collect after service?

- Which staff actions drive delays or accelerate collections?

Cash flow is not just a reporting line item. It is the oxygen your clinic breathes. Deprive it, and your clinic will suffocate slowly, but surely.

Patient Collections: The Growing Revenue Risk

High-deductible health plans are no longer an exception. They are the new normal. Historically, patient responsibility accounts for 30 to 40 percent of healthcare revenue in many clinics.

If your patients' financial experience is confusing, adversarial, or slow, you are throwing away revenue that you will never recover. The areas where you need to investigate and implement include:

Clear estimates before service.

Friendly reminders.

Transparent billing.

Easy online payment options.

Flexible payment plans.

These are your survival strategies.

If you are still operating on the old model of "send a confusing bill and hope for the best," you are committing "financial malpractice" against your own clinic.

The clinics that win the future will be the ones that treat patient financial engagement as a strategic priority, not an afterthought.

The Hidden Cost of Leadership Drift

Operational failures do not sustain themselves. They are sustained by leadership inattention, excuses, or outright denial.

Every revenue black hole that exists in your clinic today does so because someone in leadership tolerated it.

Maybe you inherited broken systems. Maybe you delegated billing oversight too far. Maybe you prioritized marketing, growth, or expansion over operational discipline.

It does not matter how the failure started. It matters what you do about it now.

Bold leadership owns reality. It confronts facts without flinching. It sets new standards and demands strict adherence.

You cannot delegate accountability. You cannot outsource leadership. You must own the health of your clinic operationally as fiercely as you own its clinical outcomes.

It is not about blaming the past. It is about seizing the future.

The Psychological Trap: "We Are Too Busy"

One of the most dangerous lies clinic leaders tell themselves is "We are too busy to fix it."

Too busy to verify insurance eligibility. Too busy to improve denial processes. Too busy to optimize patient collections.

Busy is not an excuse. Busy is the byproduct of broken processes. What is the reason people are too busy? What are they doing?

Do you need more staff? Maybe but once you expose your revenue black holes, what you will find is that staff members are not too busy to fix your revenue cycle.

The busyness is because the process has not been fixed yet. Improved processes along with automation, minimize steps, and make the work more efficient.

Operational chaos compounds over time. Every process you neglect today multiplies administrative load tomorrow.

Fix it now or spend forever chasing the consequences.

Leadership Challenge: Conduct a Revenue Black Hole Audit

Within the next seven days:

- Audit your front-end processes for eligibility, authorizations, and copay collections.

- Review your denial trends and identify the top three root causes.

- Analyze your A/R aging buckets and isolate the biggest delays.

- Mystery-shop your own patient billing experience as if you were a first-time patient.

Document the truth. No sugar-coating. No spin. No hiding.

Wherever the bleeding is happening, commit to attacking it ruthlessly by taking these actions:

Assign owners.

Set deadlines.

Demand results.

Follow up.

Make changes to improve.

The future of your clinic depends on your willingness to face the facts others would rather ignore.

The black holes are real. The bleeding is real. The opportunity to save your clinic and build something stronger than ever is real but only for those bold enough to lead.

Lead without apology. Move with urgency. Save your clinic.

The choice is yours.

Chapter 2
Diagnose or Die

The Brutal Truth About Your Revenue Cycle

You cannot fix what you do not understand. You cannot treat what you have not examined. You cannot lead what you have not diagnosed.

Just like in healthcare diagnosis, you have to understand the malady before the appropriate treatment can be administered. This is not a philosophical observation, it is the brutal truth of clinic leadership as well.

If your clinic's cash flow is unstable, inconsistent, or just plain unclear, the primary root issue is not your billing software or your EHR system. It is the absence of rigorous operational diagnosis.

We do not want your thought process to be focused on denial codes or clearinghouses in this chapter. Place your focus on your commitment as a leader to look your revenue cycle "in the eye" and confront what others avoid.

The truth is simple: **your cash flow is not broken by chance; it is broken by what you have not diagnosed.**

The Lifeblood of the Business

In medicine, the consequences of missing a diagnosis are obvious.

The patient suffers. Without treatment, delays lead to deterioration. Symptoms that seemed minor reveal themselves as markers of something fatal.

Your clinic's cash flow works the same way.

If you miss the early signs, the consequences grow exponentially. A handful of preventable denials becomes a wall of lost revenue.

An overlooked front-end error becomes a monthly cash shortage. A slow A/R turnover becomes a cash flow emergency.

All the while, the practice looks fine from the outside. People observing the patient are none the wiser as to the issues they are facing.

The schedule is full. The staff is working. The bills are being sent. To all observers, including yourself, all is well but underneath, it is bleeding.

Just like an untreated patient, it will die slowly, painfully, and predictably.

Diagnose What, Exactly?

The biggest leadership failure in revenue cycle management is failing to ask this one question regularly: **What exactly is going wrong in our clinic, and why?**

This is not a question you ask once a year. It is a question you ask every month, especially as you perform your monthly accounting activities.

Diagnosing your RCM means investigating:

- Where are claims getting stuck?

- Where is cash flow being delayed?

- What part of the process causes the most rework?

- Who owns each part of the revenue cycle and are they succeeding?

- Where do patients get confused about their financial responsibilities?

It means knowing your clinic's operational anatomy better than any outsider ever could.

Cash Flow Is Not a Department, It Is a System

Too many leaders think of revenue cycle issues as billing department problems.

That's the equivalent of blaming the nurse when a patient flatlines from an undiagnosed illness.

The billing team is critical, but they are not the only variable. They are part of a system that spans from the first patient phone call, to the final payment posted.

Diagnosing your revenue cycle means seeing the whole system as interconnected.

It means understanding that what happens at intake directly affects what happens at payment posting. It means recognizing that one breakdown upstream causes five downstream problems.

RCM is not just a function, it is the circulatory system of the entire business, and when it is not flowing, everything else begins to suffer:

Patient satisfaction

Staff morale

Growth

Sustainability

Your vision is great patient care. You will need to keep your business strong so you can achieve your vision.

The Illusion of Activity

One of the biggest reasons clinics fail to diagnose their RCM problems is that they confuse activity with effectiveness.

Claims are being submitted. Statements are being printed. Phone calls are being made.

That's good activity, but activity is not the same as productivity and accuracy. Movement is not the same as momentum.

You may be submitting 1,000 claims per month, but if 200 are denied and 50 are never followed up on, then you are leaking value and reinforcing failure.

Leadership must go deeper. You must ask not just "Is the team busy?" but "Is the system delivering results?"

Busyness can mask failure, and many clinics bleed out while everyone is working hard, but no one is diagnosing the real problems.

Rapid Front-End Precision: Where Cash Flow Begins

If diagnosis starts anywhere, it starts with your front end. The first step of the R.E.V.I.V.E. Framework is Rapid Front-End Precision for a reason.

Revenue cycle starts at the first contact with the patient whether it is by phone, email or fax. Most revenue cycle failure begins before the patient is even seen.

When your intake is sloppy, things get missed. When the patient's insurance is not verified, when authorizations are missed, when copays are not collected, everything else downstream becomes chaos.

Your billing team can only work with what they are given. If the patient's name, insurance ID, date of birth, or authorization code is wrong or missing, denial is guaranteed.

Why do so many clinics tolerate front-end breakdowns?

That's because leadership is not inspecting it or does not have any inspection system or verification system in operation.

Diagnosis begins with observation. If you have not personally walked through your intake process in the last 90 days, you do not truly know how strong or weak it is, and until you do, you are leading blindly.

Visibility Is a Leadership Tool

Diagnosis requires visibility. You cannot lead a revenue cycle you cannot see.

Leadership is about confronting the brutal facts. You must see your denial rates, your A/R aging buckets, your clean claim rates, and your patient collection rates in real time.

You must live in the numbers, not guess based on feelings, which means dashboards, reports, and audits. It also means sitting with your team and tracing the lifecycle of a claim from beginning to end. Blind leadership is like not really "seeing" your patient.

The results are that the function of leadership is sick or dead.

If you do not know how long it takes to submit a clean claim... or what percentage of claims are denied on first pass... or how long it takes to rework a denial... then you are not in command.

Diagnosis is not optional. It is leadership in motion... Leadership in Action!

The Hidden Cost of Undiagnosed RCM Problems

What does a ineffective diagnosis cost you?

It costs cash because denied claims take longer to collect.

It costs staff time because they are reworking what should have been done right the first time.

It costs patient trust because financial confusion undermines the clinical relationship.

It costs clinic growth because cash shortages prevent reinvestment.

Perhaps worst of all, it costs your team the belief that they are part of something excellent. Nothing demoralizes great people faster than being stuck in broken systems that leadership does not fix.

When you do not diagnose, you not only lose revenue, but you also lose trust.

Leadership Is Diagnosis

You do not need to be a coder. You do not need to be a billing technician, but you must be a diagnostic leader.

That means asking:

- What patterns are we missing?

- What questions are we unaware of?

- What questions are we avoiding?

- What problems are we downplaying?

- What metrics are we ignoring?

... and then doing something about it.

Real leadership is not about saying, "It's not my area, because my staff handles that."

It is about saying, "If it's bleeding revenue, it's my responsibility."

No Diagnosis, No Change

You can implement new technology. You can hire new staff. You can attend new conferences, but none of it matters if you fail to diagnose the core and then lead the change.

Just like with your patients, when you cannot diagnose the results can be disastrous.

The power of the R.E.V.I.V.E. Framework lies not in its cleverness but in its clarity.

It forces you to examine what others avoid. It gives you a structure to inspect what others tolerate, and it all starts with diagnosis. The path of diagnosis is not easy. It requires courage to stare at the areas that have not been given the appropriate level of attention.

It demands accountability from every staff member. You must get that commitment for accountability from your staff.

You do not have to fix everything at once, but you must find what is broken because the longer you wait, the worse the bleed.

In the world of RCM, delay is death.

Leadership Challenge: Diagnose Without Excuses

Over the next seven days, launch a full R.E.V.I.V.E. diagnostic sweep of your revenue cycle:

Walk through the front-end intake process. Identify any missed verifications or sloppy eligibility checks.

Pull your denial reports.

- Rank the top five causes.
- Assign ownership to fix them immediately.

Randomly audit twenty claims before submission.

Measure the clean claim rate.

List three processes you could automate within the next ninety days.

Build a simple dashboard showing your top five financial KPIs.

Staff and leadership should review these together, weekly. Have someone "Mystery-shop" your billing process as a patient. Identify friction points.

Document everything you uncover. No filtering. No minimizing. No blaming.

Confront the truth.

Real leadership demands real diagnosis.

Your clinic's future depends on whether you have the courage to look and the discipline to act.

Lead boldly. Diagnose relentlessly. Refuse to lose.

Now, take what you've uncovered and translate it into action.

Your diagnostic work is the foundation and what you do next determines everything. Create your first R.E.V.I.V.E. Action Plan.

Contact us for you **R.E.V.I.V.E. Execution Action Plan**.

It's a part of the real-world system our top-performing clinics use to transform insight into results.

You've seen what's broken. Now build what works.

Turn diagnosis into direction.
Turn direction into discipline.
Turn discipline into revenue.

Start your R.E.V.I.V.E. Action Plan now. Your clinic won't wait and neither will the future.

Chapter 3
The Heavy Price of Leadership Failure

OK, Here comes the toughest chapter and challenge … Ready?

If your clinic is bleeding revenue, although places to look include your billing software, your front desk, and your claims clearinghouse, the most important place to look is the mirror.

The core truth of this chapter is blunt but necessary: **Your revenue crisis is a leadership crisis.** That's not an insult. The body follows the head. It's a diagnosis, and diagnosis is the beginning of healing.

The chapters before and after this one are filled with systems, tactics, and strategies for strengthening the financial performance of your clinic, but none of them matter if leadership fails.

You can automate denial management, outsource collections, and track metrics with precision, but if the people at the top do not lead boldly, decisively, and visibly, the organization will stall.

Even if you automate and outsource all of the above, if you are not leading the work, how can you know it is working properly?

You are not just managing processes. You are shaping reality.

This chapter is earlier in the book rather than later because leadership either creates the environment for execution, or leadership permits the excuses that undermine it.

Your Revenue Crisis Is a Leadership Crisis

Revenue problems do not emerge from nowhere. They are the natural outcome of what leadership allows, ignores, or delays.

A leader who assumes "someone else is watching the numbers" is the **first** blind spot.

A leader who lets operational confusion persist without clarity is the **second**.

A leader who avoids hard conversations about underperformance is the **third**.

Together, those blind spots form a system destined to underdeliver.

If the cash flow is tight, if the denials are high, if A/R is aging, the problem is not just the billing team. The problem is leadership's failure to confront, correct, and command.

Revenue bleeding is the symptom. Leadership neglect is the disease.

Until this is internalized, no tactical change will stick. Fixing software, reassigning staff, or adding dashboards will only lead to short-term bumps.

Long-term transformation begins when leadership takes full, personal ownership of the revenue cycle, not as a side responsibility, but as a strategic imperative.

The Denial of Denials: Avoidance Has a Cost

Every clinic that ignores its denial rate is writing silent checks it cannot cash. It is a financial hemorrhage disguised as normalcy.

Denials not tracked are revenue never claimed. Delays not escalated are payments lost to the clock, and staff underperformance that is not corrected compounds over time.

Avoidance is not neutral. It is expensive.

You do not need to be a billing expert to know if your A/R is out of control. You just need to ask. The data is already in your system. The question is whether you are looking, whether you are leading through it, and whether you are demanding action.

If your team is not reviewing denials weekly, not resolving root causes monthly, not escalating patterns immediately, then leadership is paying the cost of inaction.

Here's the hard truth: **The cost of not fixing it is far higher than the cost of discomfort in addressing it.**

You Set the Pace or You Set the Trap

Leadership creates tempo. It sets urgency. It defines what is acceptable and what is not.

If you do not set a clear, fast pace for revenue cycle execution, you are unintentionally setting a trap.

Confusion becomes culture. Finger-pointing becomes normal. Accountability fades into the background.

When no one knows what matters most, everything feels optional.

The bold leader says, "This is the standard. This is how we move and this is how we measure."

Weak leadership looks the other way. It lets good people drown in bad processes. It tolerates delays, excuses, and sloppy handoffs, and then it wonders why results are inconsistent.

If you are not setting the pace, you are enabling the chaos.

People Follow What You Tolerate

Every habit your staff shows is a reflection of what you've accepted. Not necessarily what you've said, but what you've tolerated.

If documentation is sloppy, it's because sloppiness has no consequence. If billing tasks are delayed, it's because urgency has not been enforced. If no one follows up on aging accounts, it's because silence from leadership has replaced standards.

Sometimes people rise to the level of intention. In those cases, intention must be clear. You will need to ensure there is clarity.

This does not always happen ... people do not always rise to the levels of expectation or intention. Sometimes they fall to the level of what's allowed.

The question is not: "Does your team know the policy?"

The real question is: "Do they believe you care about it enough to enforce it?"

The loudest leadership signal may appear to be the policy manual but it's the follow-through from leadership.

The Cost of No Clear Vision

A clinic without financial direction is a clinic adrift.

If your team cannot describe what "good" looks like in financial performance, they are guessing.

If your billing lead cannot articulate expectations around your A/R goals, denial targets, or clean claim rate, then decisions are being made in a vacuum.

You know your Vision matters but not just for mission or culture but for money.

You do not need a hundred KPIs. You need clarity on what winning looks like.

Here's the bigger truth: **When you align financial strength with patient care excellence, you unlock the clinic's full potential.**

A financially weak clinic cannot expand services, reward staff, or invest in innovation; therefore, it cannot successfully offer great patient care. Financial clarity is not greed. It is good stewardship.

Misaligned Priorities: When Patient Care Suffocates the Business

There is a dangerous lie in healthcare leadership: "If we just focus on the patient, the money will take care of itself."

That is partially true, but not entirely.

Patient care and financial health are not opposites. They are co-dependent. A clinic that ignores its revenue systems in the name of compassion will eventually collapse under its own generosity, and when that happens, you and your staff lose, and ultimately, the patients lose.

You cannot serve patients well if your clinic is financially broken.

Great care requires great cash flow. Excellence requires resources. Mission requires margin.

This is not about choosing business over healing. It is about recognizing that stewardship of revenue is what allows healing to happen sustainably.

The Cost of Leadership Failure

The cost of leadership failure begins with chaos around your cash flow. Without Rapid Front-End Precision, the intake process becomes a breeding ground for revenue loss.

The failures of missed eligibility verifications, inaccurate copay collections, incomplete authorizations each bleeds cash and forces billing teams into a frantic, reactive posture.

Cash that should flow effortlessly instead clots within broken systems, starving the clinic of operational oxygen.

As cash flow weakens, the second cost appears: reputation erosion. **Patients are not always able to separate you performing your clinical duties as clinical excellence, from how your back office runs and the associated operational dysfunction.**

If their financial experience is sloppy, unclear, or hostile, they will view the entire clinic as untrustworthy. No amount of medical expertise can repair the damage done by a billing nightmare.

Patients who once trusted you to heal them will quietly walk away if you cannot handle their financial journey with clarity and respect.

Operational burnout soon follows. Staff working inside broken systems are forced to compensate for leadership's failure to enforce discipline. They spend their time fighting fires that should never have ignited. They waste energy fixing errors that should have been prevented. They miss opportunities to help the organization grow.

Over time, talented employees lose faith. They stop trying. They leave, and every departure further strains an already battered organization.

Then comes strategic paralysis. Without relentless visualization of metrics, leaders cannot see the true state of their clinic.

Decisions are made on gut feelings rather than being informed by hard data.

Fear replaces boldness.

Investments are delayed.

Opportunities are missed.

Growth plans stall.

The clinic becomes trapped in a cycle of operational stagnation, unable to move forward because it no longer knows how or where to lead.

Worst of all, leadership failure leads to mission drift and the inability to achieve the vision.

Clinics are born from vision which as you know is the desire to serve, to heal, to impact lives.

When financial chaos rules, that vision erodes. Resources for innovation dry up. Staff enthusiasm dwindles. Excellence turns into survival. Mission becomes maintenance. Dreams feel like burdens.

Leading Through Numbers: The Metrics You Can't Afford to Ignore

Strong leaders manage with data, not anecdotes.

They know their denial rates. They review their aging buckets. They track first-pass resolution on issues. They check days in A/R. They ask about net collection rates. They don't need to be billing experts. They need to be **metric-minded leaders.**

You do not inspect data because you distrust your team. You inspect data because you own the outcomes and the welfare of your team.

Dashboards are not for the billing department. They are for the C-suite, the leadership team.

When leaders lead through numbers, performance follows. Clarity increases. Accountability rises. Decision-making improves.

What you care about, you measure.

If you're not reviewing your revenue metrics weekly, you are leading in the dark.

Accountability Is the Backbone of Profitability

Everything that matters must be measured. Everything that's measured must be reviewed, and everything that's reviewed must be acted on, everything acted upon must be check to verify that the intended benefits are achieved.

That is the loop of leadership. It does not end with observation. It ends with ownership.

The clinic that has weekly RCM performance reviews, monthly billing audits, and quarterly strategic revenue meetings will outperform one that doesn't every single time.

Not because they have better staff, but because they have better follow-through.

Accountability is not harsh. It is healthy. People want to win, but they need clear expectations and honest feedback.

Ask your billing team: "What's our current denial rate?"

If they cannot answer, the problem is not them, it's the lack of leadership rhythm.

Don't Just Lead People, Also Lead the Process

You are not there just to motivate people. You need to command results.

That means you cannot stop at team meetings and emails. You must inspect the pipeline. You must walk the workflow.

You must ask: "Where do claims get stuck? What's our documentation lag? How long between denial and appeal?"

You must "walk the claim" from intake to reimbursement.

It's not micro-management. It's leadership stewardship.

When leaders understand the process, they lead with precision. When they do not, they lead with hope, and hope is not a strategy.

Your Turnaround Starts With a Mirror

There is no change without courage, and there is no turnaround without accountability.

You do not need permission to lead differently.

You need a mirror.

If revenue is broken, you fix it. If accountability is soft, you strengthen it. If your team is unclear, you lead them with clarity.

You can delegate tasks, but you cannot delegate ownership.

The clinic will not transform until the leader does, and leads the transformation.

The clinics that will dominate the future will not be the ones that only "care more." Caring more and patient care are the primary basis for your work and is your vision. These we feel you have well in hand.

The clinics that will dominate the future are the ones whose leaders also lead better. They will be clinics where operational discipline fuels financial strength, where financial strength funds mission growth, and where mission growth transforms lives.

Every day, you are choosing ... Either you are paying the heavy price of leadership failure, or you are investing in the dividends of leadership excellence.

You cannot delegate this responsibility. You cannot postpone it. You cannot wish it away.

You must decide.

You must act.

You must lead.

Leadership Challenge: Uncover the True Cost

Within the next seven days, gather your leadership team and conduct a brutal, honest assessment of where leadership failure is bleeding your clinic.

Identify where revenue is leaking due to front-end mistakes. Track the impact of denials that could have been prevented. Calculate the cost of aging A/R over ninety days. Measure the staff turnover rate and its financial impact. Survey patient satisfaction related to billing and communication.

Do not soften the numbers. Do not excuse the trends. Do not shift the blame.

Document the full cost in dollars, in staff morale, in patient loyalty, and in strategic opportunity.

Then decide: will you continue paying the price of failure, or will you invest in bold leadership that changes everything?

Face the truth. Lead with courage. Transform your clinic.

The future is waiting for a leader strong enough to claim it.

Chapter 4
Stop the Bleeding
Battle-Tested RCM Fixes

Stopping revenue leakage is not a management task. It is a leadership emergency. No successful physician would stand over a bleeding trauma patient and calmly suggest that they "monitor the situation" or "wait to see if it gets better." They would act with urgency. They would mobilize every tool and resource at their disposal. They would focus on survival first, then on healing, then on thriving.

Your clinic's revenue cycle deserves the same decisive, disciplined leadership.

Too many clinics allow small operational wounds to grow into fatal hemorrhages.

They tolerate eligibility errors because "everyone makes mistakes."

They accept high denial rates because "insurance is complicated."

They ignore aging receivables because "we are short-staffed."

They send patients confusing bills because "the software is hard to use."

Every one of these excuses is a blade carving away at your clinic's financial lifeblood. Every tolerance of mediocrity is a voluntary surrender of your mission, your growth, and your impact.

It stops now.

The R.E.V.I.V.E. Framework is your battle-tested solution to stop the bleeding, stabilize your revenue, and rebuild a financial system strong enough to fuel your future.

The first step is **Rapid Front-End Precision**. Most revenue loss begins long before a claim is submitted. It begins the moment a patient calls to schedule. If insurance verification is incomplete, if authorizations are skipped, if copays are not collected, the financial infection begins. Rapid Front-End Precision requires a mindset shift. It demands that every front-desk employee understands they are not just managing appointments. They are defending revenue. They are the first guardians of the clinic's financial health. Eligibility must be checked in real time. Authorizations must be confirmed before service.

Copays must be requested before clinical engagement. No assumptions. No delays. No exceptions.

Eliminating Denial Sources is the second pillar. Denials are not a cost of doing business. They are a report card on leadership discipline. Every denial must be treated like a system failure that could have been prevented.

Leaders must commission weekly denial reviews. Every denied claim must be classified by cause. Trends must be attacked with root cause analysis and process redesign. Training must be deployed to weak points immediately. Denial management cannot be reactive. It must be a relentless assault on waste, confusion, and error.

The third line of defense is **Verifying Every Claim Before Submission**. Claims are not harmless paperwork. They are financial demands backed by clinical action. Submitting a claim without full validation is an act of negligence. It invites denials. It delays cash. It weakens trust with payers.

Every claim must be scrubbed thoroughly. Coding must be precise. Documentation must support every service. Modifier rules must be followed. Timely filing limits must be met. Claims should move through a controlled quality assurance check, not a chaotic guessing game.

Investing in Smart Automation supercharges this effort. Automation reduces human error and liberates human judgment. Eligibility verification can be automated through real-time interfaces. Claim scrubbing can be automated with advanced edits and rules engines. Payment reminders can be triggered automatically through text, email, and portal systems.

Automation is not about replacing people. It is about unleashing them. It allows your best team members to focus on solving problems, strengthening relationships, and accelerating revenue and growth.

Visualizing Metrics Relentlessly transforms leadership from firefighting to structured control. Without real-time visibility into key metrics, you are piloting your clinic blindfolded.

Leaders must see daily clean claim rates, denial trends, accounts receivable aging, and patient collection performance. Metrics must be brutally honest. They must be integrated into daily operations, not buried in monthly reports.

Leaders must meet with their teams weekly, staring reality in the face. Good news must be celebrated. Bad news must be attacked without delay. Visibility creates accountability. Accountability creates progress.

Engaging Patients Financially Early completes the revenue defense system. Patients cannot be treated as passive participants. They must be financially prepared before clinical care begins. Cost estimates must be clear.

Payment policies must be transparent. Options for payment plans must be discussed early. Digital payment tools must be easy and accessible.

Patients who understand their financial obligations are more likely to pay, more likely to return, and more likely to recommend your clinic.

Confused, frustrated patients are a cancer on cash flow and brand reputation.

The R.E.V.I.V.E. Framework is the difference between clinics that survive and clinics that thrive.

It is the blueprint for clinics that weather regulatory storms, payer changes, and economic shocks without losing momentum. It is the system that converts operational chaos into operational confidence, but frameworks do not implement themselves.

They demand leadership action.

Stopping the bleeding is not a memo. It is a movement. It requires you to stand before your staff and declare that the old standards are dead.

Revenue leaks will no longer be tolerated, and operational excuses are over; from this day forward, precision, discipline, and accountability will rule.

You must retrain your intake teams to operate like elite units. You must rebuild your billing processes to prevent denials before they occur. You must overhaul your claim validation systems. You must invest in automation, not as an IT project but as a survival necessity. You must make your metrics as visible as vital signs in an ICU. You must transform your patient financial communications into a model of clarity and compassion.

You must lead.

Stopping the bleeding is a campaign, not a one-time fix. It is a battle fought daily. It is won through repetition, inspection, and discipline. It is sustained through culture, communication, and coaching.

You must make the R.E.V.I.V.E. principles your clinic's operational commandments. You can find the REVIVE principles within the back pages of this book.

You must embed them into your onboarding, your training, your evaluations, and your rewards.

You must not allow drift, decay, or excuses to reclaim the ground you recover.

The clinics that dominate their markets are not the ones with the flashiest ads or the newest buildings.

They are the ones whose leaders refuse to tolerate revenue loss. They are the ones who built financial fortresses strong enough to fund innovation, attract talent, and expand their impact.

They are the ones whose leaders stopped the bleeding before it became fatal.

You must become that leader.

You must choose financial health over operational comfort.

You must choose discipline over denial.

You must choose to lead.

The survival and success of your clinic depend on it.

Leadership Challenge: Launch the R.E.V.I.V.E. Offensive

So far, you have investigated what is causing the bleeding.

You have worked to diagnose the problems.

You have address issues surrounding your vision and strategy and have a team ready to commit to your leadership.

Now it is time to take the action towards transformation.

Within the next thirty days, lead your team through a full operational reset based on the R.E.V.I.V.E. Framework.

Re-engineer your front-end processes to achieve perfect eligibility, authorization, and copay collection rates.

Attack your top denial sources with immediate corrective actions and permanent fixes.

Redesign your claim submission system to guarantee verification before transmission.

Automate at least three manual revenue cycle processes.

Implement real-time metric dashboards visible to all leadership stakeholders.

Redesign your patient financial engagement materials for maximum clarity and simplicity.

Host weekly leadership meetings to review progress, surface barriers, and eliminate them on the spot.

Measure everything. Celebrate wins loudly. Address failures immediately. Refuse to backslide.

The bleeding stops when you decide it does.

The clinic rises when you lead it to.

Now is the time to act.

Now is the time to lead.

Now is the time to REVIVE.

Chapter 5
Clinics That
Refused to Fail

Case Studies in Financial Rebirth

Failure was not inevitable. It was a choice that these clinics refused to make.

The most powerful proof that financial transformation is possible lies in the real-world stories of leaders who stared down chaos, made the hard decisions, and executed relentlessly. They did not have better luck. They did not have better patients. They had better leadership, better discipline, and a better commitment to operational excellence.

They implemented the R.E.V.I.V.E. Framework with the urgency of a trauma surgeon stabilizing a critical patient and the results were not just impressive. They were transformational.

The first clinic was a mid-sized orthopedic practice drowning under its own weight. Their days in accounts receivable had stretched beyond 120. Denials averaged over 14 percent. Staff turnover was rampant. Patient complaints about billing were becoming routine. The physicians were excellent, the patient volume was steady, yet the financials were slowly suffocating the practice. Leadership was paralyzed by a belief that the problems were too big and too entrenched to fix.

That belief almost cost them everything.

When they finally decided to act, they acted with total commitment. They rebuilt their intake processes for Rapid Front-End Precision. They made eligibility checks mandatory at scheduling, not at check-in. They created clear scripts for collecting copays upfront. They retrained every front-desk team member not as an administrative worker, but as a frontline defender of revenue.

Next, they launched a full assault on denials. Every denial was analyzed, categorized, and rooted out. Coding errors were slashed through retraining and better templates. Authorization errors were eliminated by installing a mandatory verification workflow. Claims were verified before submission with a rigor they had never practiced before.

Automation followed. Eligibility checks, claim scrubbing, patient reminders all moved from manual chaos to automated consistency. Staff who once spent hours chasing data were freed to focus on solving problems and accelerating cash flow.

Leadership built visual dashboards using their EHR and billing platforms. They reviewed clean claim rates, denial rates, and A/R aging every Monday morning without fail. Visibility became cultural. Excuses evaporated.

Patients were engaged financially early and often. Estimates were provided. Options were discussed. Statements were redesigned for clarity. Staff were trained to have confident, compassionate financial conversations.

In twelve months, the clinic slashed its denial rate to under three percent. Days in A/R dropped below forty-five. Patient billing complaints fell by over 60 percent. Staff morale improved dramatically. Financial stress was replaced by operational control. Growth initiatives that had been frozen for years restarted with fresh energy.

This was not magic. It was leadership executing the R.E.V.I.V.E. system with intensity and discipline.

Another story comes from a multi-site primary care group that thought outsourcing their billing would solve everything. It did not. Their outsourced vendor processed claims but never addressed upstream failures. Denials piled up. Front-end errors multiplied. Patients were alienated. Revenue Cycle Management was treated as "someone else's problem."

It was not.

Revenue is always a leadership responsibility. You cannot outsource accountability.

This leadership team faced a choice. Blame the vendor, or fix themselves first.

They chose the harder, better path.

They took Rapid Front-End Precision seriously. They reclaimed control over eligibility verification, copay collection, and prior authorization capture. They forced their vendor to meet new, stricter standards. They implemented claim verification processes internally to catch mistakes before they left their system.

They invested in automation to ensure patient communications, statement reminders, and follow-ups ran like clockwork. Staff received metric reports daily, not monthly. Denials were triaged aggressively. Appeals were handled systematically.

Patient financial engagement moved to the forefront. Payment plans were proactively offered. Patients received clear, predictable financial communications at every touchpoint. Collections increased by 30 percent in less than nine months.

By forcing visibility, discipline, and relentless operational execution, they turned a vendor relationship that had been a liability into a partnership of strength. Their revenue performance improved beyond projections, and for the first time in five years, they were able to expand to a new location without cash flow concerns.

Again, no luck. No shortcuts. Just leadership embracing the hard work of excellence.

Another transformation story comes from a pediatric practice group that thought their small size excused inefficiency. "We are a family. We are not corporate." That was their mantra, but as deductibles rose and payer scrutiny increased, their revenue could not support their vision. Staff were stressed. Doctors were distracted. Financial conversations with parents became combative.

Leadership realized that "family" without operational strength is just dysfunction with a smile.

They adopted the R.E.V.I.V.E. mindset without apology.

Their front-end processes became non-negotiable. Eligibility. Authorizations. Copay collections. Clear scripts. Regular audits. Staff were coached relentlessly until execution became muscle memory.

Denial management became a daily discipline. Claims were scrubbed, verified, and submitted with confidence. Denials were not "handled." They were attacked.

Automation lightened the administrative load. Payment posting, reminder generation, and claim tracking all moved to systems that could be trusted to execute consistently.

Metrics were posted on the wall for every staff member to see. No hiding. No guessing. No surprises.

Patient financial engagement was reimagined as a mission of care. Clarity replaced confusion. Compassion replaced confrontation. Families paid more consistently. They recommended the clinic more readily.

In less than a year, this practice moved from barely breaking even to running at a 22 percent operating margin. More importantly, their culture shifted from apologetic to empowered. They no longer feared financial conversations. They no longer crossed their fingers when running month-end reports. They knew they were running a business that deserved to grow.

These clinics refused to fail. They refused to surrender to operational decay. They refused to live in denial about their revenue cycle weaknesses.

They chose leadership. They chose the R.E.V.I.V.E. Framework. They chose to act before collapse became inevitable.

And they won.

Your clinic can too.

But only if you stop making excuses.

Only if you stop hoping "things will get better" without serious intervention.

Only if you lead differently than the clinics that are shrinking, struggling, or shuttering today.

The R.E.V.I.V.E. Framework is proven. It is not theory. It is execution. It is the bridge between financial pain and operational power.

The clinics that survive the next decade of healthcare transformation will be those whose leaders act now with urgency, precision, and courage.

The clinics that hesitate will become case studies in failure.

You get to decide which story you will write.

You get to decide whether you will be a clinic that refuses to fail or one that fades quietly into irrelevance.

The choice is not about market conditions. It is not about government policies. It is not about luck.

It is about leadership.

It is about you.

Leadership Challenge: Craft Your Clinic's Rebirth Plan

Over the next thirty days, gather your leadership team and draft a Clinic Rebirth Plan based on the R.E.V.I.V.E. principles.

Assess your current front-end processes. Identify denial trends. Analyze your claim validation steps. Audit your automation potential. Review your metric visibility. Redesign your patient financial engagement journey.

Do not aim for "better." Aim for "excellent."

Create a written plan. Assign owners. Set deadlines. Build accountability checkpoints.

Lead this initiative personally.

Do not wait for another quarter of mediocrity to pass you by.

Create your clinic's rebirth now.

Lead like your future depends on it because it does.

Chapter 6
Build Your
Execution Machine

The Rigor that is Behind Results

There is a reason most clinics struggle to fix their revenue cycle. It is not lack of information or lacking intention. It is the brutal absence of operational rigor. Talk is cheap. Strategy decks are easy. What is hard and what separates thriving clinics from dying ones, is execution.

Execution is the arena where leadership proves itself.

You can hire experts, install new software, retrain staff, and hold motivational meetings, but if you do not build and enforce a system that works every single day, your results will remain mediocre. Your revenue will bleed slowly through operational cracks that leadership has failed to seal.

This chapter is not about motivation. It is about architecture. It is about creating a machine that does not rely on memory, mood, or meetings. It is about systems that execute flawlessly under pressure. Like an elite surgical team, your revenue cycle must perform with precision, not occasionally but always.

As you have seen in the previous chapter that the R.E.V.I.V.E. Framework, although informs strategy, it is not a strategy document. It is your construction manual. Each component is a buildable, executable layer of your operational system but only if you treat it that way.

Design for Precision

Rapid Front-End Precision is a requirement to which your team members must commit. Eligibility must be verified before the patient ever arrives. Prior authorizations must be secured without fail. Copays must be collected before services are rendered. If you tolerate shortcuts here, you have already lost.

Design intake workflows to enforce compliance. Build in checkpoints. Automate alerts. Train for precision, inspect for performance, and fire for noncompliance if necessary. The system must function without apology.

Denials Are a Failure of Leadership

You are not *Eliminating Denial Sources* if your team is constantly fixing denials.

You are not managing. You are reacting. Your job is to build a system where denials become rare exceptions. That means your team must investigate every single denial and trace it to a source. Wrong code? Missing document? Payer policy missed? You must hardwire preventive corrections into your workflows. The denial report is your operational health report. Read it like a diagnosis. Treat it like an emergency. Denials are not a billing issue. They are a leadership issue.

No Claim Should Leave Your Clinic Unchecked

Verifying Every Claim Before Submission is non-negotiable. If a claim leaves your system and gets denied for something preventable, it is bigger than just a mistake because it is operational malpractice. Build validation rules. Use scrubbing tools. Set up pre-submission audits. Create a policy that no claim moves forward unless it passes every check. This is where most revenue is lost. This is where most clinics fail. You do not need more effort. You need tighter gates.

Automate the Repeatable, Elevate the Human

Investing in Smart Automation is how you escape the cycle of chaos. Stop expecting your team to remember ten thousand micro-steps. Use technology to carry the burden. Automate eligibility checks. Automate reminders. Automate denial categorizations. Automate dashboards.

Do not fear automation. Automation is not about reducing staff. It is about increasing capacity.

When you automate the routine, your people can focus on what matters but only if leadership installs the tools, integrates them smartly, and trains relentlessly.

Make Metrics Impossible to Ignore

Visualizing Metrics Relentlessly means you stop hiding your numbers in spreadsheets and start leading with them. Your clean claim rate, denial rate, A/R aging, and patient collections must be visible every single day.

They must be part of every huddle, every staff meeting, every leadership review. Metrics, in addition to informing, they drive behavior.

If your team does not see the numbers, they will not care about the numbers. If you do not lead them in the importance of the numbers, then they will not understand the impact.

Install wall dashboards. Produce and share weekly summaries. Publish rankings. Create incentive programs to encourage improvement.

Public visibility fuels performance.

Train Your Team to Speak Financially

Engaging Patients Financially Early is not a billing department task. It is a cultural shift.

Every staff member must know how to talk about money. From the receptionist to the provider, your team must learn to speak clearly about costs, coverage, and payment options.

Patients do not hate paying. They hate being surprised. Eliminate confusion. Offer plans. Make it easy. Financial clarity is critical, and it is a competitive advantage.

Execution Is Not Optional, It Is Your Job

Building your execution machine is not something you assign to a committee. It is your job as the leader.

You must personally own the architecture. You must define the workflows, set the standards, and review the results. You must enforce relentlessly. You must build muscle memory into your team's daily actions.

Execution is not about pressure. It is about systematization and consistency. It is about making excellence the default.

Reinforce with Systems, Not Speeches

You do not need another motivational talk. You need infrastructure. Workflows. SOPs. Validation checkpoints. Audit schedules. Performance scorecards. Incentive plans. Escalation protocols. Your clinic should run like an operations command center, not a loosely managed group of well-meaning people. You do not build execution with passion. You build it with process.

Culture Follows Clarity

Operational culture is not built in retreats or slogans. It is built in how work gets done.

If excellence is measured, enforced, and rewarded daily, it becomes the culture. If shortcuts are ignored and sloppiness is tolerated, that becomes the culture.

You are not just building systems. You are training people how to think, act, and lead. Define what excellence looks like. Make it visible. Make it loud. Make it non-negotiable.

Execution Is Your Edge

The clinics that dominate their markets are not the ones with the most ideas. They are the ones who execute better than anyone else.

They train their teams like pros. They monitor their metrics like air traffic controllers. They redesign processes like engineers. They act with speed, clarity, and force. That is what your clinic must become.

You may need more meetings in accordance with what youhave learned so far but more importantly, you need machine-level execution. You need real-time accountability. You need bold action.

The R.E.V.I.V.E. Framework is your guide. Your leadership is the engine. The only thing left is your will to build.

Leadership Challenge: Build the Machine

Leadership Challenge: Build Your Execution Blueprint

Within the next thirty days, architect your execution machine and create a full operational execution blueprint for your clinic based on the R.E.V.I.V.E. Framework.

Design your intake processes for flawless precision.

Engineer denial elimination systems into daily operations and denial workflows that self-correct

Build claim validations that stop errors cold. Institute mandatory verification checks before every claim submission.

Deploy smart automation in all feasible areas. Automate everything that is repeatable.

Install real-time metric dashboards for leadership oversight. Make metrics so visible that they shape behavior.

Transform your patient financial engagement into a streamlined, proactive system.

Define ownership for every component. Establish inspection routines for every standard. Set penalties for slippage and rewards for excellence.

Train your team to lead financially.

Do not theorize. Build.

Do not discuss. Execute.

Do not hope. Lead.

Your execution machine will either become your clinic's greatest asset or your greatest regret.

Your reputation will not be built on what you say. It will be built on what you produce. Execution is the language of leadership. Start speaking it fluently.

The decision is in your hands. Lead this like it is your final legacy project. Because in many ways, it is.

Your clinic needs your machine. Start building now.

Chapter 7
Allies, Not Just Vendors

Finding Your RCM Execution Partner

In the battlefield of healthcare finance, survival is not won alone. Victory belongs to those who choose their allies with ruthless clarity and unwavering standards. The right partner can accelerate your clinic's financial performance beyond anything you could achieve alone. The wrong partner will drain your cash, destroy your credibility, and bleed your clinic dry.

This is not about outsourcing tasks. This is about forging alliances with warriors who fight beside you, not vendors who simply invoice you. It is about recruiting partners who understand the urgency of revenue capture, the non-negotiable precision of claim management, and the strategic importance of patient financial engagement.

It is about finding a Revenue Cycle Management partner who lives the R.E.V.I.V.E. Framework as fiercely as you do.

You cannot choose casually. You cannot choose reactively. You cannot choose based on promises, marketing brochures, or price alone.

You must choose based on alignment of mindset, mastery of execution, proven ability to deliver measurable results that matter and alignment to your vision.

Most clinics stumble because they confuse vendors with partners. Vendors perform tasks. Partners protect missions. Vendors meet minimums. Partners chase excellence. Vendors wait for instructions. Partners anticipate problems and solve them before you even see them.

Choosing a true RCM ally starts by demanding Rapid Front-End Precision from day one. Your partner must prove their intake systems guarantee eligibility verification before service, authorization capture without gaps, and upfront financial counseling with patients. They must show you data, not words. They must demonstrate their workflows are engineered to prevent front-end revenue wounds.

They must obsess over Eliminating Denial Sources. Your partner must not accept denials as normal. They must attack them at the root. They must provide real-time denial analytics, root cause breakdowns, and clear corrective action plans. They must be able to show you month-over-month improvements in clean claim rates, not just empty promises about "working on it."

They must treat Verifying Every Claim Before Submission as a sacred discipline. Every claim they touch must be scrubbed, validated, documented, and proofed against payer rules. Sloppy billing processes are acts of negligence. Any partner who sends claims without ironclad verification is not an ally. They are an operational risk.

They must facilitate your Investing in Smart Automation and see it as a strategic priority. Manual work creates errors. Slow work creates cash flow starvation. Your RCM partner must leverage advanced tools for eligibility verification, claims management, patient reminders, and real-time reporting. If their systems feel slow, outdated, or paper-heavy, they will drag your clinic backwards.

They must Visualize Metrics Relentlessly. A real partner makes your operational truth visible every day. Denial rates. Days in A/R. First-pass resolution. Patient collection rates. You must be able to see, question, and act on real data at any time. Partners who hide behind quarterly reports or vague dashboards are not allies. They are liabilities.

Finally, they must assist you to Engage Patients Financially Early with compassion, clarity, and competence. Your brand is on the line every time a patient receives a financial communication. Your partner must help you treat your patients as if they were their own. They must understand that financial confusion damages clinical trust. They must be able to design payment experiences that strengthen loyalty while accelerating collections.

Choosing the wrong RCM partner is one of the most expensive leadership mistakes you can make. It poisons cash flow. It creates operational chaos. It alienates staff. It drives away patients. It paralyzes strategic growth.

Choosing the right RCM partner is one of the smartest investments you can make. It stabilizes cash flow. It boosts staff morale. It strengthens patient relationships. It liberates leadership to focus on expansion, innovation, and clinical excellence.

The difference between the two outcomes is not luck. It is leadership.

You must lead the search process yourself. You must be as demanding as you would be in hiring a new surgeon. You must define the standards clearly, enforce them ruthlessly, and walk away from anyone who cannot meet them.

No compromise.

You must start by defining exactly what excellence looks like for your clinic.

Not in generalities but specifics. They will help you figure out things like, what clean claim rate is acceptable? What is the maximum allowable denial rate? What are your target days in A/R? How quickly must patient payments be posted? How often must metrics be reported?

If you cannot define it, you cannot demand it. If you cannot demand it, you cannot expect it.

Next, you must interview potential partners the way you would be hiring a key executive, not a task manager. You must ask about their methods around helping you with workflows, escalation paths, and quality assurance systems.

You must discuss governance. Demand service-level agreements with penalties for underperformance. Insist on monthly leadership meetings to review results, set priorities, and address risks. Partnerships without structured accountability decay into finger-pointing and excuses.

Above all, you must align on mindset. You are not looking for a company that "helps you with billing." You are looking for warriors who view your clinic's financial health as a mission worth fighting for. Allies who will push you to operate better, not just complete tasks faster. Partners who will challenge you when necessary, not simply nod and invoice.

The clinics that thrive over the next decade will not be the ones that choose the cheapest vendors. They will be the ones that forged alliances with world-class RCM partners who shared their values, matched their urgency, and lived their discipline.

The clinics that limp into the future, barely surviving, will be the ones that choose partners based on brochures, promises, and price tags.

The future is being written now.

You must decide what side of history your clinic will be on.

There are no neutral choices. There are only powerful allies or silent saboteurs.

Leadership is about choosing wisely, decisively, and unapologetically.

You are not hiring a vendor. You are recruiting an ally for a war that determines your clinic's future strength, growth, and survival.

Choose with eyes wide open.

Choose with standards set high.

Choose with the courage to walk away from mediocrity.

Choose partners who live the R.E.V.I.V.E. Framework every day, not just talk about it when selling you.

Your patients, your staff, and your future deserves it. You deserve it.

The difference between clinics that dominate and clinics that decline is leadership.

The difference between operational acceleration and operational decay is the quality of your allies.

Choose boldly. Choose wisely. Choose now.

Leadership Challenge: Forge Your RCM Alliance

Within the next sixty days, if you have an RCM partner, conduct a full partnership audit against the R.E.V.I.V.E. standards. Demand hard evidence of Rapid Front-End Precision, Denial Elimination Systems, Claim Verification Rigor, Smart Automation, Metric Visibility, and Patient Financial Engagement Excellence.

If gaps are found, demand improvement with clear timelines. If resistance or excuses arise, prepare to replace.

If you do not have an RCM partner and are considering outsourcing, initiate your search with the standards outlined in this chapter. Set non-negotiable expectations. Interview deeply. Inspect thoroughly. Align culturally.

Make the decision not based on price, but based on operational strength and results.

Refuse to settle. Refuse to hope.

Choose allies who will build your future with you.

Lead like it matters, because it does.

Chapter 8
Future-Proofing Your Clinic's Financial Power

The clinics that dominate tomorrow are being built today. Not through slogans or marketing campaigns, but through bold leadership decisions that hardwire financial strength into every operational fiber of the business. The future will not be kind to the unprepared. Payers will tighten reimbursements. Patients will expect more. Competition will intensify. Only the clinics that have constructed resilient, flexible, execution-driven revenue operations will survive, let alone thrive.

This chapter is not about distant trends. It is about immediate decisions that secure your clinic's long-term power.

Future-proofing your financial strength starts with total mastery of the fundamentals. No amount of artificial intelligence, automation, or predictive analytics can save a clinic that tolerates ineffective intake processes, weak denial management, or inconsistent billing execution. No technology can mask leadership laziness. No innovation can paper over a refusal to diagnose and fix core revenue cycle problems.

The foundation is and will always be Rapid Front-End Precision. No patient should move through your clinic without eligibility verified, benefits confirmed, authorizations secured, and financial expectations set. Every missed verification is a crack in your foundation. Every uncollected copay is a silent bleed that will become catastrophic over time. Future-proof clinics do not "try" to get it right. They demand perfection from the front lines every single day.

Future-proof clinics also treat Eliminating Denial Sources as an endless war, not a one-time project. They hunt denial trends before they can become revenue cliffs. They deploy root cause analysis weekly. They update coding workflows. They retrain staff at the first signs of process decay. They do not tolerate the normalcy of seven to ten percent denial rates because "that is just healthcare." They smash through industry averages and set new internal standards of operational dominance.

Verifying Every Claim Before Submission becomes religious practice in future-proof clinics. It is non-negotiable. No claim leaves their systems without passing a gauntlet of checks for coding, documentation, and payer-specific requirements. Speed does not replace accuracy. Both are demanded simultaneously. Claims are engineered to survive payer scrutiny, not to simply move through the billing conveyor belt faster.

Smart Automation is treated not as a tech project but as a strategic weapon. Future-proof clinics automate every routine task that does not require human judgment. Eligibility verification. Claims scrubbing. Patient reminders. Payment posting. Denial routing. They free up human beings to focus on critical thinking, patient engagement, and high-value problem-solving. They never allow manual processes to become bottlenecks or excuses for revenue loss.

Metrics Visibility becomes a living, breathing management system. Future-proof clinics do not wait for quarterly reports to find problems. They have live dashboards. They conduct weekly operational reviews. They inspect denial rates, A/R aging, and collection trends in real time. Leaders manage with facts, not hope. Staff know they are being measured. Culture becomes disciplined, transparent, and proactive.

Patient Financial Engagement is rebuilt into a world-class experience. Future-proof clinics eliminate financial surprises. They set expectations up front. They offer estimates that are clear and realistic. They offer digital payment options that are easy and frictionless. They follow up respectfully but relentlessly. They transform billing from a point of friction into a point of trust. They turn patients into advocates, not adversaries.

The R.E.V.I.V.E. Framework is not just a model for today's recovery. It is the model for tomorrow's dominance.

Applying the R.E.V.I.V.E. Framework today is not enough. Future-proofing requires forward-looking leadership willing to anticipate what is coming and act before the pain forces it.

The future will belong to clinics that embrace real-time financial engagement. Patients will no longer tolerate confusing, delayed bills. They will expect Amazon-like transparency and convenience. Clinics must invest in tools that provide accurate upfront cost estimates, real-time eligibility confirmation, digital payment options, and self-service billing portals.

The future will belong to clinics that leverage predictive analytics. Historical reporting will not be enough. Leaders will need tools that can predict denials before they happen, forecast patient payment likelihood, and model cash flow risks based on payer behavior changes. Leaders must upgrade their analytic capabilities or be blindsided by avoidable revenue loss.

The future will belong to clinics that build Revenue Intelligence into daily decision-making. Revenue Intelligence means integrating operational, financial, and clinical data to optimize everything from service line profitability to payer negotiation strategy to staffing models. Clinics that separate billing data from strategic planning will operate blind while smarter competitors capture market share.

The future will belong to clinics that treat their RCM vendors not as task executors but as strategic partners. Transactional vendor relationships will collapse under future pressures. Only true alliances, forged on mutual accountability, operational excellence, and shared strategic goals, will survive.

The future will belong to clinics that create Financial Resilience Funds. Revenue cycles are cyclical. Even the best clinics will face months where reimbursements slow. Future-proof clinics set aside cash reserves equal to at least three months of operating expenses. They insulate themselves from seasonal dips, payer delays, and regulatory disruptions. They plan for storms before the clouds gather.

The future will belong to clinics whose leaders live and breathe operational excellence every day, not just in times of crisis.

The decision to future-proof is a leadership decision. It is a choice to act now rather than react later. It is a choice to invest in systems, discipline, and capabilities while others cling to the illusion that "good enough" will last.

Good enough will not last.

Only excellence survives.

Only bold leadership wins.

You must ask yourself brutal questions:

Have you engineered your front-end processes to eliminate revenue wounds before they occur?

Have you embedded a denial prevention system that attacks problems at the root rather than treating symptoms?

Have you created a bulletproof claim validation process that survives payer scrutiny?

Have you deployed automation not just for efficiency but for strategic advantage?

Have you made revenue-critical metrics visible, measurable, and actionable in real time?

Have you transformed patient financial engagement into a trust-building experience?

If the answer to any of these is no, you are already vulnerable.

If the answer to most of these is no, you are already in danger.

There is no neutral position. You are either building future-proof strength, or you are passively setting yourself up for future collapse.

The future punishes leaders who wait.

The future rewards leaders who move.

You cannot hide from the future. You can only prepare for it or be broken by it.

The R.E.V.I.V.E. Framework is not an optional enhancement. It is your survival kit. It is your battle plan. It is your blueprint for building a clinic that thrives no matter what pressures come next.

The future belongs to the leaders who understand that financial health is not a function of volume, reputation, or marketing. It is a function of operational precision, relentless execution, and visionary investment.

You must choose.

You can cling to old models, slow processes, outdated mindsets, and fragile cash flow systems.

Or you can lead your clinic into a future where financial power fuels clinical excellence, mission fulfillment, and strategic expansion.

You can future-proof your clinic.

Or you can watch it wither under forces you could have anticipated but failed to prepare for.

The choice is not distant.

The choice is today.

Lead now.

Build now.

Secure your clinic's future now.

Leadership Challenge: Future-Proof Your Revenue Cycle

Within the next sixty days, develop a Future-Proofing Action Plan for your clinic.

Assess your current front-end, denial management, claim validation, automation, metrics visibility, and patient engagement systems against the standards outlined in this chapter.

Identify at least three immediate upgrades you can implement.

Identify three medium-term strategic investments you must plan for.

Document your plan.

Assign clear leadership accountability for every priority.

Set deadlines.

Start executing immediately.

Do not theorize about the future.

Build it. Own it. Lead it.

Your future is either secured by your actions today or surrendered by your inaction tomorrow.

There will be no second chances.

The leaders who act now will dominate the next decade.

The leaders who delay will disappear.

Choose to lead. Choose to win.

Choose to future-proof your clinic.

Epilog
Financial Power,
Bold Leadership,
and an
Unstoppable
Future

The journey you have undertaken through these pages is not about technical tweaks to billing processes. It is not about chasing a few extra percentage points of collections. It is not about minor operational improvements.

It is about reclaiming control over your clinic's financial destiny.

It is about stepping fully into bold leadership when others settle for mediocrity.

It is about refusing to watch helplessly as hidden operational wounds bleed your clinic of energy, resources, and purpose.

It is about deciding, finally, and without apology, that your clinic will not be a statistic. It will not be another story of slow financial collapse disguised as normalcy. It will not be a place where excuses rule and patients suffer the consequences.

You have been handed the blueprint. The R.E.V.I.V.E. Framework is more than a set of tactics. It is a philosophy. It is a system for leading clinics into financial strength and operational freedom.

Rapid Front-End Precision taught you that excellence starts before the first claim is ever filed. Every interaction at intake is a make-or-break moment. Precision there is not optional. It is survival.

Eliminating Denial Sources showed you that denials are not random storms to be weathered. They are structural weaknesses to be hunted down and eradicated systematically. Great clinics do not manage denials. They obliterate them at the root.

Verifying Every Claim Before Submission demanded that you abandon any culture of rush, shortcut, or "good enough." Claims are not paperwork. They are the financial oxygen of your business. Every one must be battle-ready before it leaves your hands.

Investing in Smart Automation revealed that technology is not a threat to your people. It is the shield that protects them from drowning in avoidable errors and low-value work. It is the force multiplier that liberates excellence.

Visualizing Metrics Relentlessly reminded you that hope is not a management strategy. Numbers do not lie. They show you whether your systems are strong or crumbling. They are the truth serum every leader needs, even when the truth is uncomfortable.

Engaging Patients Financially Early reinforced that billing is not an afterthought. It is part of the patient experience. It is part of your brand. Clinics that respect patients financially build loyalty. Clinics that confuse or frustrate patients financially destroy it.

The R.E.V.I.V.E. Framework is your operational backbone, but it requires something more than processes and dashboards.

It requires bold leadership because none of the strategies outlined in this book implement themselves.

Front desks do not suddenly become precise because a new form is introduced.

Billing teams do not spontaneously hunt down denials because a new report is issued.

Claims do not verify themselves. Patients do not automatically feel engaged and empowered.

Culture does not shift by accident. Systems do not strengthen by luck.

Only leadership creates change.

Only leadership demands better.

Only leadership transforms clinics from slow, struggling, underperforming businesses into thriving, dominant, future-proof institutions.

Leadership is not a title. It is a choice.

Every single day.

The choice to face hard truths instead of hiding behind soft comfort.

The choice to demand excellence when mediocrity would be easier.

The choice to act now rather than wait for crisis to force your hand.

The choice to measure, to inspect, to correct, to coach, to insist.

The choice to put the future of your clinic, your patients, and your team ahead of your personal discomfort, your pride, or your fear.

The clinics that will still be thriving ten years from now will not be the ones who had the slickest websites. They will be the ones whose leaders built operational execution machines so strong that no payer, no competitor, no recession, no regulation could break them.

They will be the ones whose leaders refused to settle.

The world is not getting easier for medical practices. Anyone selling you that illusion is lying. Costs are rising. Complexity is multiplying. Competition is intensifying. Patients are becoming more empowered and more demanding.

The margin for error is shrinking.

The reward for excellence is growing.

In this future, your revenue cycle is not a back-office issue. It is a strategic weapon. It funds your mission. It protects your culture. It enables your growth.

You cannot treat it as an afterthought.

You cannot delegate it blindly.

You cannot hope it works itself out.

You must own it.

You must lead it.

You must transform it.

The R.E.V.I.V.E. Framework is your starting point. It is your compass. It is your operating system.

But only you can supply the fire.

Only you can supply the discipline.

Only you can supply the non-negotiable demand for operational excellence that turns systems into results.

You have been given the blueprint.

You have been given the roadmap.

You have been shown the truth about what separates thriving clinics from dying ones.

Now the decision is yours.

Will you lead boldly?

Will you refuse to allow excuses to reign?

Will you build the systems, the culture, the execution machine your clinic deserves?

Will you future-proof your financial power?

Or will you drift back into the patterns that have silently drained so many others?

You cannot have both.

You cannot be both committed and complacent.

You cannot be both hopeful and passive.

You must choose.

Now.

Leadership does not wait.

Leadership moves first.

Leadership acts decisively.

You have the tools.

You have the insight.

You have the responsibility.

Lead with precision.

Lead with courage.

Lead with the relentless drive to turn potential into performance, ideas into execution, strategy into unstoppable financial strength.

The clinics that change healthcare for the better will not be the ones who wanted to.

They will be the ones who led like it mattered.

Because it does and now, so must you.

Leadership Challenge: Declare Your Clinic's Financial Rebirth

If you have **worked** through this book, you have work to do and now is the time. If you have done your work, then go back and review each chapter and its Leadership Challenge. Do the work. Then, come back here and make these declarations and get your Action Blueprint in front of you as the daily game plan for you and your team.

Within the next thirty days, gather your leadership team. Stand before them and declare a new operational era.

Declare that excuses are over.

Declare that precision is the standard.

Declare that every part of the R.E.V.I.V.E. Framework will be implemented fully, ruthlessly, and unapologetically.

Declare that denial of financial reality will never again be tolerated.

Declare that patient trust will be earned not just in clinical care but in financial clarity.

Declare that operational visibility is non-negotiable.

Declare that this clinic will be a fortress, not a fragile house of cards.

Draft your R.E.V.I.V.E. action blueprint.

Assign owners.

Set deadlines.

Measure progress.

Celebrate victories loudly.

Attack weaknesses ferociously.

Lead as if your future depends on it.

Because it does.

The revolution starts with you.

The rebirth starts now.

The future belongs to the bold.

Claim it… Now.

Afterword

The Future Belongs to the Bold

Every generation of leaders faces a defining moment. A crossroads where the easy path promises comfort but delivers collapse, and the hard path demands sacrifice but delivers destiny.

You, standing at the edge of this book's final words, are facing such a moment.

You did not pick up this book to be entertained. You picked it up because something inside you refused to settle. Some part of you knew that your clinic deserved more, your patients deserved better, and your staff, your mission, and your future demanded a stronger, smarter, faster way forward.

You were right.

The silent crisis in clinic revenue cycles is not an accounting problem. It is a leadership crisis. It is the inevitable consequence of tolerating excuses, allowing systems to rot, and letting fear of hard truths paralyze decisive action.

You know now that survival is not about luck. It is about execution. Thriving is not about slogans. It is about operational precision. Growth is not about good intentions. It is about relentless, disciplined, courageous leadership.

You have the blueprint. The R.E.V.I.V.E. Framework is more than a set of strategies. It is a way of leading. A way of building systems so strong that chaos cannot break you. A way of aligning people, processes, and technology so tightly that revenue flows freely, patients feel cared for, and missions expand rather than shrink.

But knowledge alone is worthless without execution.

Courage without action is just theater.

Plans without discipline are just noise.

The clinics that dominate the next decade will be those whose leaders took this moment seriously. Those who used this moment to build execution machines that crushed inefficiency, destroyed excuses, and set new standards of operational dominance.

The others will tell stories. Stories about how hard it was. How unfair the payers were. How complicated the regulations became. How they "did everything they could."

And they will fade away, believing their own excuses.

You have a different choice.

You have the choice to become the leader your clinic desperately needs.

You have the choice to lead with fire, with focus, with fearless clarity.

You have the choice to stop the bleeding, build the machine, secure the future, and dominate in a world that punishes weakness but rewards operational greatness.

This book was never meant to be safe. It was not written to flatter you. It was written to confront you. To challenge you. To strip away your illusions and hand you the tools you need to fight for your clinic's life.

Every page you have read was a call to arms.

Every strategy you have studied was a weapon.

Every leadership challenge you have been issued was a battle cry.

Now, it is your move.

You can file this book away on a shelf and tell yourself you will get around to it "someday."

You can highlight passages and feel inspired without ever translating inspiration into action.

Or you can decide, here and now, that you will lead differently.

That you will not tolerate hidden bleeding in your operations.

That you will not accept slow death by denial rates, by aging receivables, by missed patient collections.

That you will not stand by while your mission shrinks because you lacked the courage to demand operational greatness.

That you will build the systems, forge the alliances, create the culture, and lead the charge that will make your clinic financially unstoppable.

Not someday, but Now!

This world rewards boldness.

It punishes hesitation.

It forgets the cautious.

It immortalizes the courageous.

You were called to leadership for a reason.

You were entrusted with the lives, the hopes, the futures of your patients and your team for a purpose.

It was not to preserve the status quo.

It was not to manage decline politely.

It was to create and to build.

It was to dominate in a world where only the strong survive and only the visionary thrive.

Your clinic's future is waiting for you to act.

Your team is waiting for you to act.

Your patients, though they may not know it, are waiting for you to act.

And the longer you wait, the narrower your margin becomes.

The future is coming faster than you think.

The competitors are getting smarter than you realize.

The patients are expecting more than you are currently delivering.

The regulators are tightening faster than you are prepared for.

Waiting is death. Action is life.

You have everything you need to move.

You have the knowledge.

You have the strategies.

You have the blueprint.

All you need now is the decision.

The decision to be bold.

The decision to be ruthless in the pursuit of operational excellence.

The decision to build a clinic so financially strong, so operationally precise, so patient-centered and disciplined that nothing – not payer tactics, not market shifts, not staff turnover, not economic downturns – can break you.

This is not hype.

This is reality.

And it is waiting for you to own it.

Lead with boldness.

Lead with clarity.

Lead with the conviction that your clinic's best days are not behind you – they are ahead of you.

But only if you seize them.

Only if you fight for them.

Only if you lead as if everything depends on it, because it does.

The R.E.V.I.V.E. Framework will not fail you.

Your team, when led with vision and courage, will not fail you.

Your mission, when backed by operational excellence, will not fail you.

The only failure possible now is the failure to act.

And that failure is a choice.

Make a different choice.

Make the choice to dominate.

Make the choice to thrive.

Make the choice to build a clinic so operationally strong, so financially powerful, so mission-driven that it stands as a beacon for others who are still lost in excuses.

This is your moment.

This is your call.

This is your time.

Lead boldly. Lead now.

Your future is waiting.

Claim it.

THE R.E.V.I.V.E. PRINCIPLES

The R.E.V.I.V.E. Framework is more than a model. It is a mindset. These are the governing principles every bold clinic leader must adopt:

1. Revenue is a Leadership Responsibility. If the numbers are broken, leadership must own the fix. No more finger-pointing, no more waiting. Your cash flow reflects your command.

2. Execution Beats Intention. Strategy is nothing without action. Talk is cheap. Execution builds resilient clinics.

3. Visibility is Power. What you cannot see, you cannot lead. Track everything. Share the truth. Lead from clarity, not comfort.

4. Precision is Protection. Every missed eligibility check or loose process is a financial wound. Protect your clinic with discipline on the front lines.

5. Urgency Wins. Time kills revenue. Every day of inaction is another day of compounding loss. Speed, not perfection, saves the clinic.

6. Accountability is Culture. What you tolerate becomes your culture. What you inspect becomes your standard. Build teams that fear missed metrics more than tough conversations.

7. Simplicity Drives Adoption. Complex systems collapse under pressure. Make it easy to follow the process, impossible to ignore results.

8. Automation Is Not Optional. Labor alone cannot fix revenue. You must install smart systems to scale precision and consistency.

9. Patients Are Partners. Treat patients as financial stakeholders from day one. Transparency earns trust. Clarity drives compliance.

10. Leadership Must Go First. You are the example. You model the urgency. You carry the weight. Your team rises or falls based on your standard.

These are the principles that power clinic transformation. These are the beliefs that drive lasting profitability. These are the truths behind every revived practice.

Live them. Lead with them. R.E.V.I.V.E. your future.

Partner with Revive Revenue Services

If you have made it to this point, you already know the truth. You already understand what is at stake. You already feel the weight – and the privilege – of leadership.

You have committed to mastering your revenue cycle. Now it is time to step forward. Now it is time to step up. Now it is time to execute with expert precision. Now it is time to REVIVE your clinic's financial future.

You were never meant to walk this leadership journey alone. You were never meant to wage war against payer complexity, operational inefficiency, and financial fragility without world-class allies beside you.

That is why Revive Revenue Services exists.

Revive Revenue Services is built for leaders like you—clinic executives who refuse to let financial dysfunction stand in the way of operational excellence and patient care.

We are not just a billing company. We are not another outsourced vendor chasing claims. We are your RCM execution partners.

We live the R.E.V.I.V.E. Framework every single day.

We do not theorize about operational excellence. We execute it.

We do not make excuses. We deliver results.

We believe that financially strong clinic teams transform patient lives, staff careers, and community futures.

We believe that the difference between survival and domination comes down to one thing: leadership that is willing to act.

If you are ready to act, we are ready to build something extraordinary with you.

If you are ready to eliminate denial chaos, slash aging receivables, unlock hidden revenue, and liberate your leadership team to focus on growth instead of survival, then it is time.

Time to stop hoping for better.

Time to stop tolerating hidden losses.

Time to stop apologizing for demanding excellence.

It is time to lead boldly. and to build operational dominance.

It is time to REVIVE.

If you are ready to:

- Slash your denial rates

- Shrink your accounts receivable

- Modernize your billing operations

- Maximize collections without sacrificing patient satisfaction

- Future-proof your revenue cycle with automation and AI

Then, Revive Revenue Services is ready to partner with you.

Visit us at ReviveRevenueServices.com and take the next step.

Connect with our leadership team. Schedule an executive financial strategy session. Ask about powerful clinic revenue tools. Access resources that extend and expand everything you have learned in this book.

This is not the end of your journey. It is the beginning of your transformation.

If you are willing to lead, we are willing to fight beside you.

If you are willing to act, we are willing to execute with you.

If you are willing to demand excellence, we are willing to deliver it relentlessly.

Do not let this moment slip away.

Do not let the fire you feel fade into another "good intention" shelved by busyness.

Move while your vision is clear and strike while your conviction is "hot". The future will not wait and neither should you.

REVIVE your clinic's financial power now.

Visit reviverevenueservices.com now.
Your next era of leadership starts today.

Revive Revenue Services. Revive your revenue. Reclaim your future.

About the Author

Flora Sanders is a transformational leader and trusted advisor to clinic executives who refuse to accept financial mediocrity.

As the founder of Revive Revenue Services, Flora brings a relentless focus on operational excellence, financial discipline, and execution power to healthcare practices.

With decades of expertise in healthcare revenue cycle management, business operations, and strategic leadership, Flora has helped clinics of all sizes break free from inefficient systems, recover lost revenue, and unlock new levels of growth and sustainability. Her work combines real-world experience, cutting-edge technology solutions, and a no-excuses approach to results.

Flora believes that financially healthy clinics deliver better patient care, create stronger teams, and have a greater impact on their communities.

Her mission is simple but uncompromising: equip healthcare leaders with the strategies, tools, and mindset necessary to build financially unbreakable organizations.

Through Revive Revenue Services, leadership engagements, and thought leadership, Flora continues to inspire clinic owners, practice managers, and healthcare executives to take bold control of their future.

Her driving philosophy is clear: Financial strength is not optional. It is the foundation for everything your clinic aspires to achieve.

To learn more, visit ReviveRevenueServices.com to access exclusive tools and leadership resources.

Revive Your Clinic Revenue

Bold Leaders: Stop the Bleeding, Crush Denials, and Build Financially Unbreakable Practices

You now have the execution plan to move your clinic forward. Will You Act or watch the "patient" deteriorate?

Denials. Delays. Dwindling cash flow. Silent killers are draining clinics every day while leaders look away, hope for improvement, and slowly lose everything they built.

Hope is not a strategy. Leadership is.

Leverage the R.E.V.I.V.E. Framework, a proven system to unleash cash flow and build a revenue cycle so strong it fuels your mission for years to come. Take action so you can lead your clinic with "surgical precision".

The future belongs to bold leaders.

Will you claim it or surrender it?

Visit ReviveRevenueServices.com to access exclusive tools and leadership resources.